D1117341

Ocean Animals

By Sandra Donovan

Raintree Steck-Vaughn Publishers
A Harcourt Company

Austin • New York
www.raintreesteckvaughn.com

Published by Raintree Steck-Vaughn Publishers,
an imprint of Steck-Vaughn Company.

Library of Congress Cataloging-in-Publication Data
Donovan, Sandra.
Ocean Animals / Sandra Donovan
p. cm. -- (Animals of the Biomes)
Summary: Discusses the physical characteristics, behavior, and habitat of various animals that live in the ocean biome.
Includes bibliographical references (p.).
Contents: Animals in oceans -- The brown pelican -- Zooplankton -- The walrus -- Sea clams - What will happen to oceans? -- Quick Facts.
ISBN 0-7398-5689-8 (hc); 0-7398-6409-2 (pbk).
1. Marine Animals--Juvenile literature. [1. Marine animals. 2. Marine ecology 3. Ecology.] I. Title. II. Series.

QL122.2 .D65 2002
591.77--dc21

2002067910

Printed and bound in the United States of America
1 2 3 4 5 6 7 8 9 10 WZ 05 04 03 02 01

Produced by Compass Books

Photo Acknowledgments
Digital Stock, cover, 6, 13, 27; Image 100, 1; Corbis, 8, 14, 40, 42, both on 45; Comstock, 11; David M. Phillips, 16; T. E. Adams, 18; Frank Aubrey, 20; Visuals Unlimited, 23; Thomas Kitchin, 24, 28, 44; Don W. Fawcett, 30; Kjell Sandved, 23; Daniel W. Gotshall, 35; Ken Lucas, 36; John Forsythe, 39, 45.

Content Consultant
David Julian
Department of Zoology, University of Florida

This book supports the National Science Standards.

Contents

Animals such as these emperor penguins live out their lives in and near the ocean biome.

Animals in Oceans

About 70 percent of Earth's surface is ocean. When you look at the world from space, it looks blue. This is because of all the oceans covering the surface.

Oceans are one of Earth's biomes. A biome is a large region, or area, made up of communities. A community is a group of certain plants and animals that live in the same place. Oceans are one kind of biome. In fact, oceans are the world's largest biome. Other biomes include forests and deserts.

Oceans are made of saltwater. This means that the water contains at least 4 percent salt. If you taste ocean water, you can easily taste the salt.

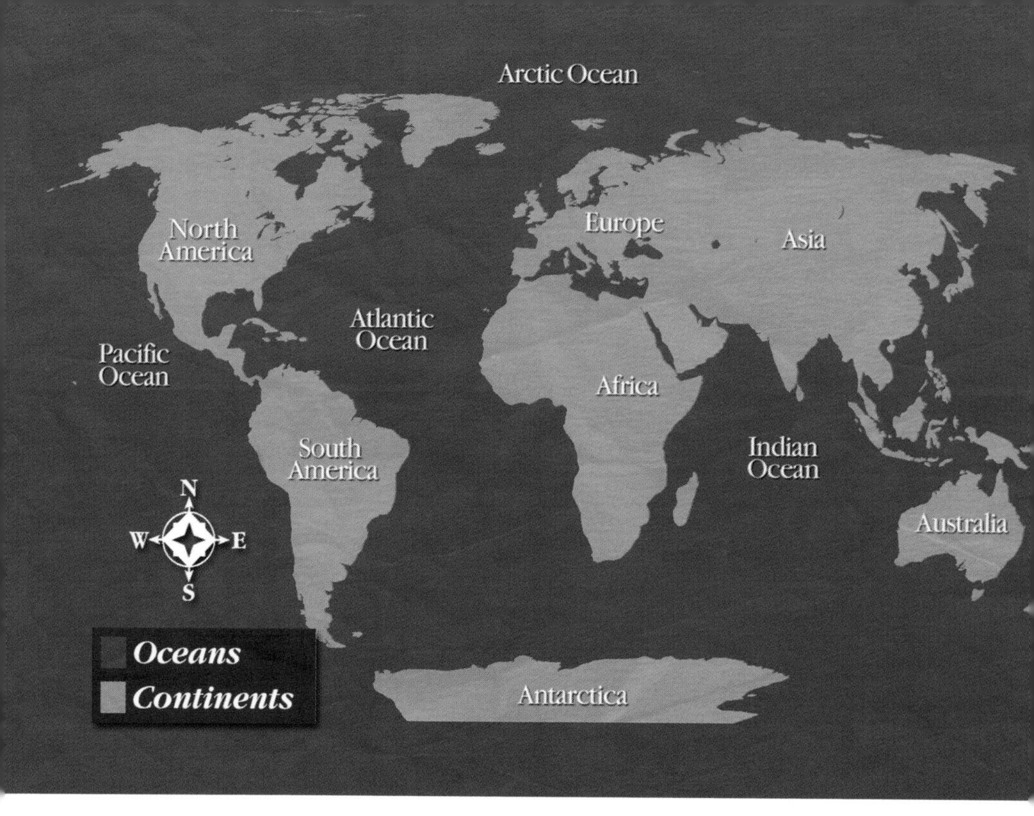

This map shows where oceans are located around the world.

What Lives in Oceans?

Many different plants and animals live in the ocean biome. Some of these like warm ocean climates, and some like cold ocean climates. Climate is the usual weather of an area over a period of time. It includes the amount of rain or snow, the temperature, and the wind.

Tropical ocean regions are near the equator. The equator is like a belt that circles Earth around its middle and divides it into two halves. The land and water near this belt are called the tropics. Tropical oceans are always warm and clear on the surface. Many plants and animals live in these tropical waters.

The areas near Earth's north and south poles are called the polar regions. Here the ocean is so cold that it freezes on the surface. Huge chunks of ice called icebergs float in these waters. Plants and animals that are adapted for life in the cold enjoy the polar regions.

Outside of the polar regions, the surface water of the oceans is warmer. Deep down, however, the oceans are cold, dark, and still.

In the chapters that follow, you will learn about four different kinds of animals that live in the oceans. Birds called brown pelicans live near ocean coasts. Zooplankton are the smallest of all the world's animals and live throughout the world's oceans. Walruses are **mammals** that live in the polar regions. Sea clams are ocean animals that live in shells.

The pouch on this brown pelican is red. Pouches can also be green or black.

The Brown Pelican

The brown pelican is a kind of bird. Birds are warm-blooded animals that have a backbone, wings, feathers, and a beak. Warm-blooded animals have a body temperature that stays more or less the same, no matter what the temperature of the air or water around them. Most birds can fly, but not all animals that fly are birds. Brown pelicans can fly.

The scientific name for the brown pelican is pelecanus occidentalis (peh-leh-CAYN-us ock-see-DEN-tal-is). Pelicanus means "pelican" and occidentalis means "west."

A brown pelican has a huge bill with an expandable pouch in it. Expandable means the pouch can get bigger when it needs to.

Using the Pouch

Brown pelicans use their expandable pouch for two reasons. One reason is to dip it in the water to catch fish to eat. The other reason is to keep themselves cool. The pouch works like a vent that allows heat to escape the bird's body.

Brown pelicans are medium-sized birds. They are about 50 inches (125 cm) tall. When their wings are stretched out, they are about 6.5 feet (2 m) wide.

Just as their name says, brown pelicans are mostly brown. When they are young, they are brown everywhere except their undersides, where they are white. When they are adults, they also have white around the head and neck.

Where Do Brown Pelicans Live?

Brown pelicans live in North and South America. They can be found in the southern United States, in the countries of Central America, and in northern Brazil and Chile in South America. They live on both the Atlantic and the Pacific oceans.

Ocean coasts are the natural habitat of the brown pelican. A habitat is a place where an

These are white pelicans. They spend winters along ocean coasts, but are also found living in and near freshwater lakes and ponds.

animal or plant usually lives. Brown pelicans like the shallow water along ocean coasts. They especially like to find sheltered bays along the coast. Sometimes they also live on islands in the ocean. Every once in a while, people find brown pelicans living near lakes instead of the ocean.

How Have Brown Pelicans Adapted to Live in Oceans?

Brown pelicans are well adapted for life in the ocean biome. They move north and south as the seasons change. During warm seasons, brown pelicans that live north of the equator move farther north to keep cooler. When the weather gets cold again, the birds move south. Brown pelicans that live south of the equator move farther south to keep cooler and north when the weather gets cold again. This is called **migrating**.

Brown pelicans have webbed feet. Webbed means that the toes are connected by skin. Webbed feet work like paddles to make it easier for pelicans to swim in the water.

Brown pelicans need to build their nests on land. They build their nests on the ground or in low trees. They use their legs to walk on the ground. To get from the water to the land and back, pelicans use their wings and fly.

What a Brown Pelican Eats

Brown pelicans have an amazing way of hunting for food. They dive into the ocean head

Sometimes pelicans fly very close to the ocean surface when they are hunting for fish.

first. They may dive from as high as 60 feet (18 km) above the ocean. When they are in the ocean, they fill their big bill with fish. Then they lean forward to drain out the water. Finally, they toss their head back and swallow the fish whole.

When they migrate, pelicans often fly very high up, where the air is thinner. Their long wings move slowly but propel them quickly.

Brown pelicans eat almost any kind of fish they can catch. Most times these are small fish, such as smelt. Sometimes they also eat shrimp or crabs if they can catch them.

A Brown Pelican's Life Cycle

Male brown pelicans gather sticks and dirt needed to make a nest. Then the female builds the nest. Sometimes the nest is just a shallow hole scraped into the ground. Other times it is a large tree nest built out of sticks.

Brown pelicans mate once a year. Then the female lays about three eggs in the nest. Both the male and female keep the eggs warm until they are ready to hatch. This is called **incubating** the eggs.

After one month, the eggs hatch. Young brown pelicans live with their parents for about five weeks. After that, they gather in a group of other young brown pelicans. This group is called a **colony**. A colony is a group of the same kind of animals that live together.

The parents still bring them food while they live with the other young birds. Both parents feed their children. Young brown pelicans usually learn to fly by about 10 weeks. Soon after that, they can start looking for food on their own.

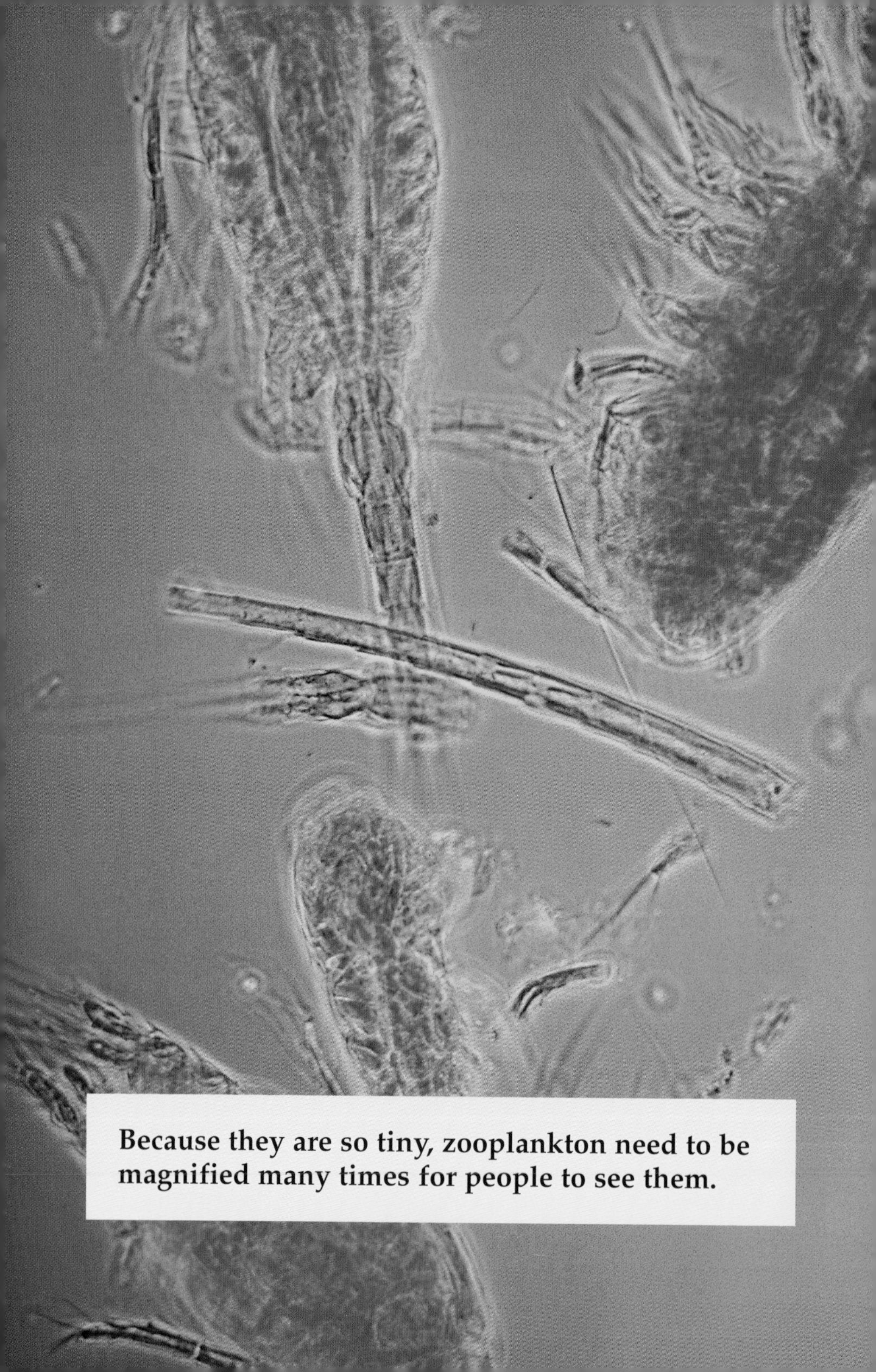

Because they are so tiny, zooplankton need to be magnified many times for people to see them.

Zooplankton

Zooplankton is the name for many different species of **microscopic** ocean animals. Microscopic means too small to be seen with the eyes. Zooplankton are some of the smallest animals in the world.

The word "zooplankton" comes from two Greek words. Zoon is the Greek word for "animals." Plankton is the Greek word for "wanders." So zooplankton means "wandering animals."

Though there are many species that make up zooplankton, there are two main kinds. One kind spends its whole life as zooplankton. The other kind grows into another small animal, such as a snail or crab.

If you were swimming in the ocean, zooplankton like this one might be all around you, but you would not be able to see them.

Copepods

The most common type of zooplankton is called a copepod (KO-peh-pohd). This word also comes from two Greek words. Cope means "oar" in Greek. Pod is the Greek word for "foot." So copepod means "oar foot." It is called this because it uses its feet to tread water.

Copepods look like tiny shrimp. They have many tiny feet. Most copepods can see only light and dark. Copepods' antennae can be longer than the animals themselves.

Where Do Zooplankton Live?

Zooplankton live in every ocean. They are the most common animal in the world. In fact, some scientists think that there are more zooplankton in the world than all other animals combined.

Zooplankton move around in the ocean a lot, but they do not move from side to side. Instead, they move up and down. A zooplankton lives its whole life in one up-and-down, or **vertical**, area called a column. Columns move from side to side because the ocean water is always moving. But the zooplankton only propel themselves up and down.

How Have Zooplankton Adapted to Live in Oceans?

During the day, zooplankton travel down deep in their column. When it starts to get dark, zooplankton move up toward the ocean's surface. This is where they find their food.

The tiny legs on this zooplankton are sticking out from the top of its body.

Predators

Because they are so small, zooplankton are not easily found by predators. Predators are animals that eat other animals for food. Zooplankton have small young. Because they are hard to find, many will grow to be adults. Some zooplankton also have spines and other sharp body parts that keep predators from eating them.

Copepods are able to swim a little because they have tiny legs. Some copepods attach themselves to bigger ocean animals. Then they move wherever this animal moves.

What Zooplankton Eat

Zooplankton are a very important part of the ocean's food chain. The food chain is the normal cycle of living things eating other living things in nature. Zooplankton are the second stage in the food chain. The very first stage is another kind of plankton, called phytoplankton (FYE-tow-plank-ton). Phytoplankton do not eat anything. Instead, they use energy from the sun to change gases in the water into food that the zooplankton can eat.

In turn, other animals eat zooplankton. Some birds, fish, insects, and mammal eat zooplankton. In fact, some species of almost every kind of ocean animal eat zooplankton. Most of these animals are small, but some are very big. For instance, whale sharks eat zooplankton, and they are 60 feet (18 m) long.

Copepods are so tiny that they have to kick their legs very fast in order to move at all. They kick their legs as much as 600 times in one minute. This uses a lot of energy, which means they must eat a lot. Every day, they have to eat as much food as they weigh. Even though they are tiny, this is a lot of food to have to eat.

The Life Cycle of Zooplankton

Because zooplankton are made of many different kinds of microscopic ocean animals, each kind of animal has a different life cycle. They grow at different rates, eat different foods, and have different life spans.

In general, all zooplankton begin life in an egg. After they hatch, they grow into adults. Some species grow large and are no longer considered zooplankton. They grow up to become snails, crabs, or other ocean animals. Some remain microscopic and are considered zooplankton all their lives.

Climate change can affect a zooplankton's life cycle. If the water becomes too warm or cold, the zooplankton may die. Pollution can

Predators that eat zooplankton swallow water and then digest any zooplankton that happen to come with it.

also affect zooplankton. **Polluted** water is water made dirty by people's actions. Zooplankton will die if the water they are in becomes polluted.

Because walruses use their tusks as tools, they have thick, strong neck muscles.

The Walrus

Walruses are mammals. A mammal is a warm-blooded animal with a backbone. Mammals give birth to live young and feed them with milk from their own bodies.

Walruses belong to the **pinniped** (PIN-ee-ped) family of animals. A family of animals is a category that scientists use to describe animals that have things in common. Pinni means "wing" or "fin," and ped means "foot." So pinnipeds are mammals that have fins that act like feet. Seals and sea lions are also pinnipeds.

Walruses have four fins and they walk on all four. Other pinnipeds use only the front two to walk. Then they have to drag their hind ends around.

Tusks

The first thing you notice on a walrus are its tusks. These are actually huge teeth that are made of ivory. On male walruses they can be 4 feet (1.2 m) long. On females they grow to be about 2 feet (61 cm) long. Walruses also have large whiskers and wrinkly skin. This skin is thick and it protects the walrus.

Walruses are usually pink or light brown. Male walruses weigh about 2,000 pounds (900 kg). Females weigh about one-third less than males.

Where Do Walruses Live?

Walruses live in the Arctic region. They live in the cold water of the Arctic, northern Pacific, and northern Atlantic oceans. They also live in seas near Russia called the Bering Sea and the Chukchi Sea.

These oceans and seas in the polar region have ice floes in them. An **ice floe** is a large, flat area of ice floating on water. These areas of ice move around in the oceans. They get smaller during the warmer weather and grow larger during the colder weather.

This walrus is using its tusks to help lift its body out of the water.

Walruses like to live in the shallow water near these ice floes. In fact, the ice floes help walruses to migrate. Walruses migrate in the spring and the fall. They do this to move to where there is more food available. Since the ice floes move in ocean, the walrus can follow them.

Walruses live close together in groups, so they must learn how to get along with one another.

How Have Walruses Adapted to Live in Oceans?

Even though walruses migrate, they spend their whole lives in the cold polar-region water. A thick layer of body fat under their skin, called blubber, protects them from the cold.

Besides digging for food, walruses use their tusks for many things. They use them to pull themselves up out of the water. They can use them to break through the ice so they can breathe. Male walruses also use their tusks to fight for mates.

Walruses are excellent divers. They can hold their breath for as long as 17 minutes, but usually come up for air every 9 minutes or so. Their heartbeat slows down when they dive, so that they use less oxygen and can stay under the water longer. Oxygen is a substance found in air that most animals need to breathe. Walruses also have a strong hind flipper that moves them quickly through the water.

Walruses use their huge tusks to dig up shellfish hiding beneath the sea bottom.

What a Walrus Eats

Walruses spend much of their day looking for food. They eat clams, snails, crabs, shrimp, and worms. They use their huge tusks to dig up food from the bottom of the ocean.

Walruses can dive 300 feet (91 m) to dig for food. They use their whiskers to feel around for food. Then they blow on the food to loosen it or to move it to where they can reach it. They eat a lot. One walrus can eat 300 clams a day.

A Walrus's Life Cycle

Walruses usually mate in February or March. The young walruses are not born for almost one year. Young walruses are called calves. They can weigh from 85 to 140 pounds (38 to 63 kg). They are a dark gray-brown when they are born.

You can tell how old a walrus is almost the same way you can tell how old a tree is. On a tree, you count the rings that make up the trunk. On a walrus, you could count the rings that form its teeth, but you would have to slice the tooth to do this. Walruses can live to be about 35 years old.

Giant sea clams live in oceans all around the world. They can be many different colors, and if stood on end would be about 5 feet tall.

Sea Clams

Sea clams are mollusks. The word "mollusk" means "soft" in Latin. Mollusks are animals that have a soft body and usually a shell. Most mollusks also have a single, strong foot. Some mollusks have tentacles instead of a foot. Tentacles are long arms, like those of an octopus. In fact, an octopus is a mollusk. Other mollusks are squid, snails, oysters, and scallops.

There are three main kinds of mollusk. One kind is called the stomach-foot mollusk. These actually have their stomach in their foot. A snail is a stomach-foot mollusk. Another kind of mollusk is the many-plated mollusk. Its body is made up of eight different hard segments, like plates.

Bivalves

Clams belong to the group of mollusks called bivalves. Bi means "two" and valve means "shell." Bivalve means "two shells." All bivalves have two shells that close together on one side. Besides clams, bivalves include oysters, scallops, and mussels.

Clams can be many sizes but they are usually between .5 inch (1.2 cm) and 4 inches (10 cm) long. But one kind of clam can grow to be huge. The giant clam is almost 5 feet (1.5 m) long. It can weigh nearly 500 pounds (227 kg). Clams can be almost any color.

Where Do Sea Clams Live?

Sea clams live in oceans all over the world. Many different kinds of sea clams live around the Atlantic and Pacific coasts of North America. They live as far north as Canada and as far south as the Gulf of Mexico. The giant clam lives in the Pacific and Indian oceans.

The ocean floor is the natural habitat of the sea clam. It lives in the sand and mud. It uses its foot to dig into the ocean floor.

This sea clam is using its foot to burrow into the ocean floor.

Some sea clams, like the giant clam, live in coral reefs. These are areas in the ocean where animals called coral lose their exoskeletons, making huge and beautiful structures. Coral reefs look like rock. The coral, which the reefs are made of, live on the top layer of exoskeletons. Coral reefs are found in tropical parts of oceans.

This sea clam's bright orange tentacles allow it to sense things happening around it.

How Have Sea Clams Adapted to Live in the Ocean?

Sea clams are protected from predators by their shells. They make their shells through a part of their body called the mantle.

Sea clams have a foot that they use for digging. They have two long tubes that they use for eating and breathing. These tubes are called siphons. They use their foot to dig down into the sand. Then they use their siphons to reach up into the water above them. These siphons start in the clam's mantle and reach out through its shell.

A sea clam's siphons are like small hoses that water can flow through. One siphon brings water into the clam's gills. The gills are small organs with microscopic hair on them called cilia. Water coming in moves across the cilia. These hairs then trap tiny pieces of food. This is called filter feeding, because the hairs act like a filter. The second siphon carries the water back out of the clam.

What a Sea Clam Eats

Sea clams eat tiny plants and animals called plankton. They eat both phytoplankton and zooplankton.

Sea clams are an important part of the ocean's food chain. After sea clams eat plankton, they become an important food for many other animals in the oceans.

The Food Chain

Many kinds of fish eat sea clams. Some of these fish, such as flounder and cod, are then eaten by people. People also like to eat sea clams. Many people in the United States and Canada eat fried clams or make a soup called clam chowder.

A Sea Clam's Life Cycle

Clams reproduce without really knowing it. Cells from the male and from the female are released into the water. When these cells meet, a tiny young clam starts to be made. This young clam is called a larva. The larva floats around in the water until it finds a safe place to grow. Usually, this place is on the ocean's bottom or on a piece of coral.

Larva are considered zooplankton and do not look very much like adult clams. They have not yet begun to make their shells. Many larva are eaten by predators. It can take from 5 to 16 weeks for the larva to grow shells. The time that it takes depends on the kind of sea clam.

These wavy-shelled sea clams live together on the ocean floor in a group called a colony.

Different kinds of sea clam grow at different rates. Even the same kind of sea clam will grow at different rates in various areas of the ocean. Some kinds of sea clam live longer than others. In Alaska, razor clams are known to have lived for 18 years. Other types of clam are thought to live for many decades.

Scientists use helicopters to study ocean animals. This helicopter is landing on ice in a polar region of the ocean biome.

What Will Happen to Ocean Animals?

The ocean biome provides a special habitat for the animals that live in and near it. Many plants and animals could not live anywhere else but in the saltwater provided by the ocean biome.

One of the main dangers to the ocean is pollution. Plants and animals die when oceans become polluted. When ships carrying oil sink or leak, fish and birds and mammals get coated with the oil. Many of them die.

Global warming is also a danger to oceans. Even very small changes to the temperature of water in the ocean can affect the life cycles of many plants and animals living there.

This humpback whale is one of the endangered animals trying to survive in the ocean biome.

How Are Ocean Animals Doing?

Brown pelicans have been endangered for a long time. Endangered means in danger of dying out as a species, or becoming extinct. In the early 20th century, people often hunted brown pelicans.

Many people have worked to help save the brown pelican. They passed laws saying that people cannot hunt as many of them. Today, there are more brown pelicans than there were 50 years ago. In many places, they are no longer endangered.

Zooplankton, in general, are not in any immediate danger of dying out. However, in parts of the ocean where the water has gotten too warm, zooplankton are no longer found in large numbers.

Walruses have been in danger from hunters for a long time. The United States passed a law against walrus hunting in 1972. The law was called the Marine Mammal Act. It said that only native people in Alaska could hunt walruses. Since then, there are more walruses and they are no longer in danger of dying out.

Most sea clams are not in danger of dying out because they are able to live in several parts of the ocean. They reproduce easily, so even when people catch many of them to eat, there are many more in the ocean.

Quick Facts

Walruses can sleep while they swim. They have sacs in their throat that they can fill with air. This makes them float on the water. Then walruses can rest with their head bobbing on top of the water while they float along.

The U.S. government passes laws that make wildlife refuges. A wildlife refuge is an area where animals can be protected from hunters and other enemies.

The very first U.S. wildlife refuge was made to protect brown pelicans, almost 100 years ago, in 1903. It is an island in Florida where brown pelicans can live and not be hunted. It is called Pelican Island. Since Pelican Island was made a refuge, brown pelicans are doing much better.

Clams can make pearls when sand gets trapped inside their shell. They cover the sand with the same substance the shell is made of. This substance builds up and creates a pearl.

Glossary

colony (KAH-lohn-ee)—group of the same kind of animals that live together in the wild

ice floe (ICE FLOW)—a large, flat-surfaced area of ice floating in water, found in the oceans of the polar region

incubating (IN-kew-bay-ting)—protecting eggs until they are ready to hatch

mammal (MAM-uhl)—a warm-blooded animal that has a backbone, breathes air, and gives birth to live young

microscopic (my-crow-SCOP-ick)—too small to be seen with the human eye alone

migrating (MY-gray-ting)—moving in response to a change in seasons or a change in the availability of food

pinniped (PIN-ee-ped)—the family of mammals to which the walrus belongs

polluted (puh-LOO-ted)—dirtied with waste from human activity

vertical (VUR-tuh-kuhl)—upright, or straight up and down

Addresses and Internet Sites

National Aquarium in Baltimore
501 East Pratt Street
Baltimore, MD 21202

U.S. Fish and Wildlife Service
Endangered Species
400 Arlington Square
18th and C Streets, NW
Washington, D.C.
20240

Conservation International
1015 18th Street, NW
Suite 1000
Washington, D.C.
20036

Sea World
www.seaworld.org

Monterey Bay Aquarium
www.mbayaq.org

Books to Read

Lalley, Patrick and Lalley, Janet. *Ocean Scientists.* Austin, TX: Steck-Vaughn, 2001.

Steele, Christy. *Oceans*. Austin, TX: Steck-Vaughn, 2001.

Index